VOL.3

7803

JOURNAL OF ARMORED
ASSAULT
& HELIBORNE WARFARE

CONCORD
PUBLICATIONS COMPANY

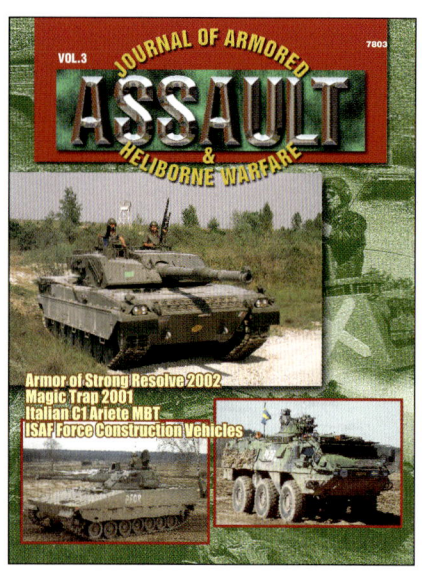

Editor: James R. Hill
Copyright © 2002
by CONCORD PUBLICATIONS CO.
603-609 Castle Peak Road
Kong Nam Industrial Building
10/F, B1, Tsuen Wan
New Territories, Hong Kong
www.concord-publications.com

We welcome authors who can help expand our range of books. If you would like to submit material, please feel free to contact us.

We are always on the look-out for new, unpublished photos for this series. If you have photos or slides or information you feel may be useful to future volumes, please send them to us for possible future publication. Full photo credits will be given upon publication.

ISBN 962-361-069-6
printed in Hong Kong

Armor of Strong Resolve

Crisis Response Operations Exercise

Yves Debay

Among the fleet of CV 90 variants deployed to Poland by the Swedish Battalion were some CV-90 armored recovery vehicles, one of which can be seen here. The vehicle has a weight of 22 tons and a crew of four soldiers. Mounted on the front of the vehicle is a stabilizer blade that can also be used as dozer blade. The vehicle has two winches with a total pulling capacity of 72 tons. A light crane is also fitted on the vehicle. For self-defense, the vehicle is fitted with a 7.62mm machine gun and 12 smoke dischargers. (Carl Schulze)

NATO in Search of a Second Wind

The end of the Cold War could have signified for NATO its programmed disappearance, or at least the end of the organization as an established armed force on the ground. The great East-West clash was fading away at a speed that no one could have predicted a few years earlier. Most of the countries that made up the Atlantic Alliance would experience a series of restructuring within their armed forces, which would certainly mean the extinction of 2/3 of their manpower and equipment.

In the long run, this policy could have led to an implosion within NATO and to its abolition as the military spearhead of the West. Add to this the irritation of certain countries, newly freed from the Soviet threat, who would have been able to distance themselves from an alliance that had no more reason to exist and, it must be recognized, was marked by the leadership and policy of Washington.

The milestone events of the 1990s would nevertheless lead to an in-depth restructuring of NATO, which, being threatened with disappearing, would evolve favorably and wind up growing from the crisis of existentialism caused by the dissolution of the Warsw Pact. The succession of crises resulting from the disintegration of the former Yugoslavia would demonstrate the limits of UN interventions. It is under the colors of NATO and by force that UN resolutions would be applied in the Balkans . . . a zone that in theory is outside the jurisdiction of NATO. The campaign waged against Serbia, and the subsequent events in Kosovo, demonstrated the solidarity of the Atlantic Alliance, which has never seemed so strong. Even countries like France that are usually "rebellious" united as a single entity behind the banner of the Atlantic crusade.

Another defining factor of the last decade that contributed to the strengthening of NATO is the desire of a number of former Warsaw Pact nations to join the Alliance. This contribution of "new blood" from small nations and mid-sized powers, diminished by 50 years of communism and enthused by the Western model, would surely be grist for the American mill. The form would be followed with the creation of the Partnership for Peace (PFP). This was a regrouping of the former Warsaw Pact nations, the Baltic countries, the traditionally neutral countries, and certain ex-Soviet republics, of which the armed forces are considered incompatible with NATO standards but have the potential to achieve them. In 1999, Poland, Hungary and the Czech Republic took the first step to leave the anteroom of the PFP and join the Alliance.

It is in Poland, a new nation to be affiliated with the Alliance, and Norway, one of the geographic pillars of the Alliance, that Exercise Strong Resolve would take place in 2002. The exercise is designed to test the application of an intervention of combined forces (CJTF), a new concept to help face threats of modern times.

The Evolution of the Alliance

The NATO concept of combined operational forces (NATO CJTF: Combined Joint Task Forces) was born during the summit of the Atlantic Alliance in Brussels in 1994. It was inspired by the American doctrine of the US Joint Task Forces, but it was applied to the 19 nations of the Alliance.

The creation of this new concept resulted simply from the political changes created by the disappearance of the Warsaw Pact and the collapse of the Eastern Bloc. New situations arose that heralded the emergence of numerous crises that were harmful to the stability and peace of Europe. To face up to it, NATO had to adapt and create a whole arsenal of responses suited to the dimension of potential crises.

One of the lessons learned in the Balkans is to use main battle tanks in peacekeeping operations for deterrence. This Leopard 2A4 from the Austrian Panzerbataillon 14 attached to Task Force Comet under Austrian command.

TASK FORCE COMET

STRONG RESOLVE 2002

Task Force Comet, as the Austria-led battle group was called, consisted mainly of forces from the Austrian 4th Panzergrenadierbrigade (mechanized brigade). The task force was named after the brigade's comet insignia. With a contribution of 510 Austrian soldiers, Exercise Strong Resolve 2002 saw the largest deployment of Austrian soldiers abroad, as well as the first deployment of Austrian main battle tanks outside Austria, since World War II. In addition to staff personnel in all command levels of the exercise and exercise control, the participating Austrian forces consisted of two tank companies with Leopard 2A4s, a mechanized infantry company with 10 Saurer armored personnel carriers, a mixed mechanized reconnaissance platoon, an armored engineer platoon with two Greif AEV and two Saurer armored personnel carriers, and an HQ and logistic support company that fielded three M-88 recovery vehicles and countless trucks. In addition, Austria provided the staff for the HQ of the 4th Multinational Brigade. (Carl Schulze)

At the time of the Cold War, it was essentially Article 5 of the Atlantic Charter that determined possible interventions by the Alliance. The meaning of Article 5 is extremely simple. It can be summarized as follows: An attack against a single member of the Atlantic Alliance is considered an act of aggression against all of its members and will be countered with the general mobilization of the armed forces of all the countries against the aggressor. The style is resolutely determined, but defensive.

The appearance of new threats would lead the political and military leaders of NATO to create the concept of CJTF in order to have another means of intervention other than Article 5. While Article 5

A total of 19 Leopard 2A4 main battle tanks from Panzerbataillon 10 were deployed to Poland. Here two of the tanks are seen at a VCP (vehicle checkpoint) in the ZOS (zone of separation) between Woodland and Treeland territory. Austria received its 114 Leopard 2A4s from the Netherlands in 1999. (Carl Schulze)

The platoon of four tanks is in charge of a roadblock. Because of their peacekeeping role, the Austrian tanks are not camouflaged and show the flag.

is perfectly adapted to the East-West conflict, it did not leave the Alliance any possibility of intervening in a sector other than that of member countries. A staff officer declared to us, "Before the adoption of the CJTF, one had to be content with watching a neighbor's house burn and intervening only if the flames touched ours."

The Alliance decided they would be able to gather non-permanent forces from NATO's reservoir to intervene other than in the territory of the Alliance to conduct missions as varied as humanitarian assistance, peace

Also under command of Task Force Comet was a mixed reconnaissance platoon formed of troops from Panzeraufklärungskompanie 4 (armored reconnaissance company) of the 4th Panzergrenadierbrigade. In addition to one section with two Kürassier Jagdpanzer, the platoon deployed two sections with two Pinzgauer 710 light trucks each. Here one of these sections returns from a "show of force" patrol. (Carl Schulze)

The machine gun seen in the turret of this Leopard 2A4 is a Belgian FN MAG, but the Austrian Army normally uses the MG-3 machine gun.

A Pinzgauer light truck of the 4th Panzergrenadierbrigade reconnaissance company. Note the MG-3 machine gun and the Task Force Comet sticker on the windscreen.

maintenance, intervention, and possibly forceful defense, in the event of a call for help from a member country of the PFP. Three large NATO commands: Regional Commands North and South and the Command of the Striking Fleet Atlantic (CSFL – Commander Striking Fleet Atlantic) would be appointed to carry out CJTF operations.

Simultaneously Carrying out Two Types of Operations on Two Fronts
Strong Resolve 2002 is part of a cycle of live exercises on the ground involving real troops (LIVEX) that take place every four years by which one can measure the degree of NATO's preparedness to face a crisis situation. This type of exercise, carried out on a full-size scale, will prove that NATO is capable of reacting when threatened on two different fronts.

The Strong Resolve exercise of 2002 was to be divided into two large-scale operations. The first is a conventional conflict played out in Norway in accordance with Article 5 that would witness the NATO countries

Mounted on the turret of the Finnish SISU is a Degtyarev 12.7mm "Douchka" machine gun.

Troops belonging to a Finnish Jäger battalion protect a meeting of Treeland partisans during Strong Resolve 2002. The soldiers are armed with the Valmet M-76 assault rifle, which is an updated version of the AK-47. They were transported by the Patria SISU wheeled armored personnel carrier seen here.

rushing to the aid of one of their own members who is being attacked by a neighbor trying to appropriate natural resources. Member countries of the PFP would also participate in the intervention into Poland.

The second portion of the exercise is a Crisis Response Operation (CRO) that will be described in more detail in this article. The dimensions of the Strong Resolve exercise can be better comprehended by looking at the number of participants: 14,000 for the Article 5 action in Norway and 26,000 for the CRO in Poland.

The scenario for the exercise, which is described in a booklet that was distributed to the participants, is reminiscent of the crisis in the former Yugoslavia. Two imaginary entities, Woodland and Treeland, once formed the prosperous union of Granica in the 1980s. Following the death of the president, Granica seemed ready to implode and divide into two nations. Treeland enjoyed a social democratic government based on the Western model, while a military junta disguised as a democracy governed Woodland. Ethnic, religious and economic problems separated the two states. Woodland dedicated 25% of its budget to defense whereas Treeland, suffering from a corrupt administration, neglected its armed forces.

Using the excuse that it had to protect its minorities, Woodland attacked Treeland in November 2000. The international community condemned the invasion. Under this pressure, Woodland asserted that its armed forces would only remain in the regions where its minorities were present. The two countries accepted the arbitration of the UN and decided

This photograph shows to advantage the profile of the SISU wheeled APC used by the Finnish Jäger battalion during the Strong Resolve exercise. The Jäger battalion is one of two units of this type attached to the Pori Brigade that make up the Finland Rapid Reaction Force.

Since Poland is a former Warsaw Pact nation, the Polish Army still uses a large amount of Russian equipment. Here a BMP-1 infantry fighting vehicle is employed as a roadblock at the firing range in Wedzryn.

This Polish BMP-1 belongs to the 12th Mechanized Brigade. The brigade is composed as follows: one staff battalion, one reconnaissance company on BRDM-2s, two mechanized infantry battalions on BMP-1s, one tank battalion on T-72s, one artillery battalion on 2S1 122mm self-propelled howitzer, and one logistic battalion. The brigade, with its 900 soldiers, has a battalion ready to serve as a UN rapid reaction force.

on a cessation of hostilities. Nevertheless, the conflict caused a serious humanitarian crisis that affected more than 400,000 impressionable refugees who were actively worked upon by their respective parties.

Given the scope of the crisis, the Secretary General of the UN, invoking Chapter VII of the Charter of the United Nations, asked NATO to conduct a CRO operation. The Secretary General of NATO charged the two main commands, SACLANT (Supreme Allied Commander Atlantic) and SCAEUR (Supreme Allied Commander Europe) to activate one combined multinational force (CJTF) to resolve the conflict and possibly oppose the powerful Woodland army.

The multinational combined force would basically act in conformance with the following plan that was applied in Bosnia:

-D + 120: after the decision to act: involvement and deployment of troops.
-D + 169: creation of a Zone of Separation (ZOS) of 2 x 2 km between the belligerent parties.
-D + 180: creation of an Extended Zone of Separation (EZOS) of 2 x 25 km between the belligerent parties.
-D + 210: creation of new borders.

Belonging to the artillery of the 7th Brigade based at Slupsk, this 122mm 2S1 "Gvodzika" self-propelled howitzer was seen at the Drawsko Pomorski training area acting as Woodland forces. During Strong Resolve 2002, PFOR troops were tasked with monitoring and controlling the movement and activities of Woodland and Treeland forces. In addition, PFOR escorted convoys back to their barracks to prevent clashes between different ethnic groups. (Carl Schulze)

Units of the 16th Division, 2nd Brigade and 7th Brigade of the Polish Army deployed with their armored vehicles during Strong Resolve 2002 and acted as Woodland and Treeland forces. Here a Polish-built T-72M1 conducts an unannounced exercise in order to provoke a reaction from the Danish peace force units whose AOR is in the Drawsko Pomorski region. The T-72M1 is armed with a 125mm smoothbore gun and a coaxial 7.62mm PKT machine gun. The vehicle in this photo is not fitted with the common turret-mounted 12.7mm NSV heavy machine gun. (Carl Schulze)

A platoon of BRDM-2s belonging to the Reconnaissance Company of Poland's 12th Mechanized Brigade stands ready for action against an angry Woodland crowd.

This brief plan demonstrates well that NATO has lost its role in a strictly defensive alliance to become a tool in crisis management, a fact that raises a debate since it seems to involve intervening into nations and altering borders for the benefit of minorities. While this latter objective may arise from a desire for justice, modifying borders in Europe can cause chain reactions that could once again spell disaster for the continent. If the cases of Kosovo and Bosnia have set legal precedent, why wouldn't Hungary be justified in claiming the area of Rumania as its own where the Magyares minority lives? And why not question the Oder-Neisse border between Poland and Germany? The debate is still open, but ten years after the Cold War, tensions are far from being calmed in a Europe that is incapable of building militarily since it refers to NATO to manage its internal crises.

In light of this, and because there is no other credible system in Europe, it is necessary for us to recognize the efficiency of the organization of the Alliance, with Strong Resolve 2002 being a completed application of it.

On the ground, the challenge raised is to test the collective mechanisms of defense and response to crises and to enhance the interoperability of the armed forces of the countries engaged. As to the latter goal, Strong Resolve was a life-size test considering the countries that participated in it. For NATO there was Germany, Belgium, Czech Republic, Denmark, Spain, France, Greece, Italy,

This close-up photograph of a Polish BRDM-2 shows how barbed wire is strung around the hull of the scout car to keep angry civilians from climbing aboard. The command vehicle version of the BRDM-2 is fitted with a special frame antenna that is somewhat similar to those used on German vehicles in World War Two.

Polish soldiers of the 2nd Company, 1st Mechanized Battalion are ready to go into action against Woodland rioters who are demonstrating to express their outrage over the destruction of their church by some unknown commando.

Norway, Netherlands, Poland, Portugal, United Kingdom, Turkey, and the USA; and for the PFP: Austria, Bulgaria, Estonia, Finland, Latvia, Lithuania, Rumania, Slovakia, Slovenia, Sweden, Ukraine, and Uzbekistan.

The US Navy in the Baltic

The crisis reaction exercise was commanded from aboard the USS *Mount Whitney* (LCC/JCC 20), a command vessel that is unique in the world and which is used as a platform for COMSTRIKFLTANT (Commander Striking Fleet Atlantic: CSFL), a rather clumsy acronym for the staff of SACLANT. A total of 98 ships would be operating in the Baltic Sea, a small number of which would portray the fleet of Woodland. Also present in the exercise would be the amphibious vessel USS *Tortuga*, which would welcome to her dock the fast assault crafts of the famous Swedish Coastal Rangers.

If the general exercise would be commanded from the USS *Mount Whitney*, the ground operations as such would be managed by the Multinational Corps Northeast (MNC NE) commanded by the Polish General Zygnunt Sadowsky. This army corps composed of three divisions (Danish, German and Polish) replaces the old LandJut (Land Jutland) of the Cold War. The MNC NE would take charge of the PFP countries so as to integrate them into the NATO units for the exercise.

An Impressive Deployment

The plan was for Poland to be divided into various zones of responsibility (ZOR), each under the command of a contingent. Operating

at Drawsko Pomorski, the large camp in the district of Pomerania east of Stettin, will be the Danish multinational brigade, including the Danish Rapid Reaction Brigade, the Swedish Crisis Reaction Battalion, and a multinational battalion made up of troops from the Ukraine, Bulgaria and the Baltic states.

Wedrzyn, west of Poznan, would welcome, under the command of the 12th Polish Mechanized Brigade, a company from the 3rd Belgian Para-commando Battalion, a Czech paratrooper platoon, and a Solvenian military police platoon.

Zagan, an enormous firing range located in Silesia, is the domain for the duration of the exercise of Task Force "Comet" under the command of the Austrian 4th *Panzergrenadier*. Under its command is a battalion from the Finnish rapid reaction force, a Slovakian platoon and a Rumanian platoon.

A Czech-French brigade and a German brigade will be represented virtually on the ground.

Along with these highly rated conventional forces, we add a Special Forces group that comprises different teams under the command of French General Poncet, commander of the COS (*Commandement des Opérations Spéciales* – Special Operations Command).

The exercise was designed so that all of these different contingents would be confronted with a variety of situations ranging from law

Travelling down a road between two lines of Polish soldiers is a Tarpan 4x4 vehicle fitted with loudspeakers. They are used to give orders to the crowd and to project shrill and irritating noise with the intent of dispersing the crowd.

Not wanting to neglect the Air Force during Strong Resolve 2002, the PFOR deployed a few missile batteries, such as this SA-3 Goa SAM battery from the Polish 91st Missile Air Defense Division, which is normally based at Obrany Rakietowy.

A Polish SA-3 Medium Range Air Defense unit of the 91st Missile Air Defense Division came under the command of the Danish Rapid Reaction Force's Squadron 543 during the exercise. Here one of the unit's launchers containing four SA-3 Goa missiles is seen mounted on the chassis of a T-55 main battle tank. The SA-3 surface-to-air missile has a range of more than 18km (11 miles) and can engage targets up to an altitude of 18km (11 miles). (Carl Schulze)

enforcement to conventional combat. Anti-riot operations were particularly spectacular and OPFOR, which was composed of Polish soldiers, did their best to rattle the nerves of the allied servicemen on their interposing missions. Several troops were injured, but the executives of Strong Resolve 2002 planned for organized fraternization sessions to lower tension following the very physically exerting exercises.

Every scenario played out corresponded to actual situations faced by SFOR and KFOR in the Balkans. For example, in Wedrzyn, an angry crowd of people from Woodland who were incensed by the burning of a church vented their anger against soldiers of PFOR that were, in theory, charged with protecting them. The uprising, which lasted for more than three hours, featured a realistic increase in intensity. Women protesting

The SA-3 missile system has been modernized and adapted to the NATO standard under the name S-125 "Newa" used by the Polish.

This is a BOV armored vehicle used by the Slovenian Military Police platoon that is attached to the Polish task force. After its independence in 1991, Slovenia was one of the first countries to receive clearance to join the PFP.

The quality of the small Slovenian Army is on the level of the armies of the NATO nations. It sends an MP platoon to each of NATO's large exercises.

An Iltis-Bombardier light 4x4 belonging to the recce squadron of the 3rd Parachute Lancers Regiment of Belgium's Para-Commando Brigade. The vehicle is armed with a MAG FN machine gun.

with their children soon gave place to Rambo types who were active in contact sports and who did not want to treat gently the soldiers in riot gear manning the roadblock.

In Drawsko Pomorski, Leopard 1 tanks and Danish VTT M-113s intervened to prevent the forces of Woodland from carrying out an unauthorized maneuver. The clash led to combat, with aircraft eventually intervening.

The large size of the Polish military camps allow the NATO forces to carry out live firing and maneuvers without being subject to the environmental constraints of Western Europe. Dutch, British, German, and American troops regularly train in Poland. However, these bilateral exercises do not reach the scale of Strong Resolve. Strong Resolve will remain the premier multinational exercise of its magnitude conducted on a full-size scale in a former Warsaw Pact nation and which is based on a realistic subject that allows a newly revitalized Alliance to apply on the ground new its doctrines of intervention.

During Strong Resolve 2002, the paratroop company of the 3rd Parachute Lancers Regiment was under Polish command in Wedrzyn. The Beligan para-commandos have an excellent reputation and are considered some of the best troops in NATO.

The oldest armored vehicles involved in Strong Resolve 2002 were three BTR-60s detached from the 1st Mechanized Battalion of the 15th Mechanized Brigade of the Bulgarian Army. For the duration of the exercise, the unit was included in the multi-national battalion of the Danish task force.

The crew of the BTR-60 consists of a driver, a 14.5mm KPV gunner, the vehicle's commander, and eight soldiers. Here one of the soldiers takes aim with his AK-47.

VS91 During Exercise Strong Resolve 2002, the Danish armed forces deployed a "Batmobil" outside Denmark for the first time. Belonging to the Rapid Reaction Force Squadron 543, the Batmobil is a mobile radar system that constantly delivers updated pictures of the air space above the AOR of the Danish Reaction Brigade. Throughout the exercise, information was also directly transmitted to the USS Mount Whitney in the Baltic Sea in order to provide SHAPE with an up-to-date air space situation report. (Carl Schulze)

The BTR-60 has a road speed of 80 km/h (50 mph) and a cross-country speed of 40-50 km/h (25-31 mph).

VS92Rapid Reaction Force Squadron 543 from Denmark is a medium-range air defense unit equipped with the Hawk air defense missile system. The unit deployed six launchers to Poland, one of which can be seen in position in this photo. Behind the launcher to the right, the TAS (Tracking Adjunct System) is visible. In the background to the left, the Multi-Role Survivable Radar (MRSR) can be seen. The version of the Hawk that is currently in use will soon be replaced by the upgraded D-Hawk variant. (Carl Schulze)

An unusual view of a Danish Hawk battery from Rapid Reaction Force Squadron 543 in travelling position. Trucks made by Magirus are used to carry the missiles.

This trailer holds three ready-to-fire Hawk missiles. In some cases three other missiles are carried on the rear platform of the truck.

If the Bulgarian BTR-60 is the oldest armored vehicle involved in Strong Resolve 2002, the Danish Piranha is the most modern and sophisticated. Here in the woods of the large training area of Drawsko Pomorski, Danish Piranhas await the order to move out. The Piranha III, nicknamed "The Fish" by its crew, is largely appreciated by the soldiers for its comfort and technology, including air conditioning, an oil burner, and individual seats with suspension for all members. The optical aiming device allows the 12.7mm heavy machine gun to hit targets from a distance of 1200 meters (1312 yards). Its road speed is 120 km/h (75 mph).

Mowag Piranha IIIs of the Danish Royal Hussars Guard prepare to lend support to an anti-riot action.

This photograph provides a good study of the large size of the Piranha III compared to the average soldier.

A total of 3500 Danish soldiers took part in Exercise Strong Resolve 2002. The exercise placed under Danish control the PFOR task force based in Drawsko Pomorski, which included the Swedish Battalion (SWEBAT) and the Multinational Battalion. This is a close-up of the Piranha III.

Under a cool rain, Piranha IIIs and troops of the Danish Royal Hussars Guard move out to confront Woodland rioters. The Royal Hussars Guard is a large, well-equipped force attached to the Danish International Brigade, which could be attached to the Multinational Corps Northeast.

The Royal Hussars Guard is a mechanized regiment organized into two battalions, a tank battalion and a mechanized battalion. The latter consists of four companies of Piranhas and one company of M-113s. Each company has three combat platoons of three vehicles.

Eighty-eight Danish Army M-113s took part in Strong Resolve 2002. Except for the storage box at the rear of the hull, there is nothing externally new about the M-113. It is, in fact, the A3 with the new diesel engine. Unlike the M-113s used in the Balkans, the M-113 of this exercise is not fitted with additive armor.

Among the large fleet of armored vehicles deployed to Poland with the Danish Reaction Brigade was a number of M-113A2 APCs fitted with the Otobreda T-25 two-man turret. The turret is fitted with a 25mm Oerlikon cannon and a coaxial 7.62mm machine gun. Denmark purchased 50 M-113A2 APCs of this type. (Carl Schulze)

Also among the Danish troops of the Rapid Reaction Brigade that deployed to Poland were four Leopard 1A5 main battle tanks of the 4th Tank Squadron. Here one of the Leopard 1A5 fitted with a dozer blade reacts to unannounced movements by Woodland armor. Exercise Strong Resolve 2002 provided the Danish tank soldiers with the opportunity to engage their former enemy of the Cold War, the feared T-72 M1 main battle tank. (Carl Schulze)

The Leopard 2 is slowly replacing the Leopard 1A5 in the Danish Army. Nevertheless, the Leopard 1A5 will probably still be in service for a couple of years. This one belongs to the Royal Hussars Guard.

The tank battalion of the Danish Army consists of three tank companies and one M-113 company. The tank company has three platoons of three tanks each. Note the camouflage net around the gun barrel and turret of this Leopard 1A5.

Along with the Danish Leopard 1A5, the most powerful vehicle involved in Exercise Strong Resolve 2002 is the Swedish CV-90 (Combat Vehicle 90). Attached to the Danish Task Force at Drawsko Pomorski, the 3rd Swedish Battalion (called Viktor-Niklas, or VN) forms the core of the Swedish Battalion, which could be used as a model of a rapid reaction force.

SWEBAT is composed of units from the following regiments: Jämtland Rifles based at Östersund, Life Guards based at Kungsängen (Stockholm), Gotland Regiment based at Visby, Noorland Dragoon Regiment based at Arvidsjaur, and the Swedish Helicopter Wing based at Linköpen. Here a CV-90 is travelling at speed.

Two platoons of Swedish CV-90s are ready to go on patrol. The first vehicle is the Forward Artillery Observer version, which is going out with the other CV-90s to organize fire support or an air strike.

A column of CV-90s is seen on the muddy tank track of Drawsko Pomorski. The Swedish Battalion consists of three mechanized infantry companies, a HQ Company, and a Combat Service Support Company. A Swedish military police platoon was attached to the Battalion during exercises in Poland.

The main combat vehicle in the Swedish Battalion is the CV-90. Along with the British Warrior, the Hispano-Austrian Uhlan/Pizarro, and the Russian BMP-3, the CV-90 is one of the most powerful AIFVs in the world.

This view of a Swedish CV-90 shows the silhouette of the vehicle's main weapon, a 40mm Bofors gun. The gun, which is fed from three eight-round magazines, has a range of 2000 meters (2186 yards) against targets on the ground and a range of 4000 meters (13,124 feet) against targets in the air.

Nice view of a CV-90 at the Drawsko Pomorski range. Note the position of the mudguard and the vehicle's name on the barrel. Both A and C Companies of the SWEBAT are fully mechanized. The company consists of three platoons with three CV-90s in each platoon.

This CV-90 is being worked on beneath a maintenance shelter. All modern armies are now using temporary buildings for maintenance and logistic operation. The Swedish vehicle is having one of its tracks repaired.

The Swedish CV-90 IFV has a crew consisting of a driver, gunner and commander. It normally carries a rifle section of eight soldiers in the rear compartment.

Sweden has acquired a large number of MT-LB armored personnel carriers from the former East German Volksarmee. They are used to perform different duties and can be used as a Battalion Command Post or, like the one seen in the foreground, as a recovery vehicle. In the Swedish Army, the MT-LB is called the Pbv401.

A side view of the CV-90 armored recovery vehicle. One of these is attached to each Swedish mechanized company.

Four Patria SISU wheeled armored personnel carriers are in service with the Swedish EOD platoon attached to the mechanized battalion of the Rapid Reaction Brigade. The shield is used to protect the user of the Barrett M82A1 .50cal sniper rifle, which is sometimes used to detonate land mines.

This photo offers a good look at a Patria SISU XA-203, which is known as the Pbv203 in the Swedish Army. It is modified with new armor and the turret of a Pbv302 tracked APC.

From their Patria SISU XA-203, soldiers of the Swedish Life Guards observe a Woodland forces camp during Exercise Strong Resolve 2002. The PFOR troops were kept busy during the active phase of the exercise ensuring that Treeland and Woodland forces that were still deployed in the field respected the peace agreement. Another mission for PFOR was to escort the troops and prevent clashes between the different forces when they had to cross each other's territory while returning to their barracks. (Carl Schulze)

A Swedish SISU XA-203 helps to guard a checkpoint. Note the soldiers of the Life Guards Regiment.

This armored BV-206 attached to the Combat Service Support Company is being used as an ambulance. The two letters "XN" are the call sign of the company

MAGIC TRAP 2001

Walter Böhm

" Old Ironsides Lands". A mechanized infantry platoon from Charlie Company, 2-6INF rolls its ODS Bradleys into attack position near the town of Wahnwegen. The "Doghouse", the armored box on the turret roof that contains the gunner's Integrated Sight Unit (ISU), was improved in 1996.

Introduction

Mechanized infantry soldiers fight dismounted to clear the way on the battlefield so their own combat units can carry on with their mechanized warfare. When a tactical situation forces mechanized troops to dismount from their vehicles and operate as real infantry, it is very important to a successful operation to have enough soldiers with effective firepower on the ground. Combat situations like the clearing of obstacles or fighting in blind terrain requires a large number of infantry and a great deal of time.

But most importantly, the firepower and physical strength of every infantryman is used up very quickly during a dismounted fight. Armored combat troops must take advantage of their superior mobility and fight mounted on their vehicles whenever possible.

The ability of mechanized units to carry out a combat order depends on three main factors: 1) the performance of their combat vehicles, 2) the capability to force the enemy from a dismounted to a mounted fight, and

"Magic Trap 2001" was the first open terrain FTX of the 2nd Iron Brigade Combat Team since 1989. Here some M2A2 ODS Bradley vehicles of B Company, 2-6INF travel to a refuel point at the cemetery in the town of Steinbach. The vehicle in front is fitted with the MILES II training system, and the following vehicle is fitted with the Precision Gunnery System (PGS) gunfire simulator.

Some M2A2 ODS Bradleys of Bravo Company played the OPFOR role during Exercise "Magic Trap 2001". These Bradleys were fitted with the PGS (Precision Gunnery System) gunfire simulator for this exercise. The PGS system is very similar to the AGDUS simulation system used by the German Bundeswehr.

This M2A2 ODS Bradley belongs to 1-6INF, the sister unit of 2-6INF. Both battalions are under the command of the 2nd Iron Brigade Combat Team. Unlike the M3A2 ODS (the version for the Cavalry units), the MICV (Mechanized Infantry Combat Vehicle) M2A2 ODS has uparmored sprocket gear boxes. The barbed wire on the engine access door was used during the night to build a fence around the vehicles.

The fuel tank of a M2A2 ODS Bradley has a capacity for 662 liters (175 gallons) of fuel. Here an Oshkosh 10-ton (8x8) HEMTT M978 "Fueler" truck fills Bradleys with JP8 fuel. The driving range of an M2A2 ODS is up to 400 km (248 miles). The Cummins engine has a fuel consumption of 165 liters (43.5 gallons) for a distance of 100km (62 miles). The M978 is fitted with two fuel pumps, so two vehicles can be refueled by the same time.

3) the reliability of their own combat support units. There should be no doubt, the punch of modern armored combat units is only as effective as the firepower and readiness of the infantrymen escorting them.

Main Battle Tanks Stopped by Bad Weather

To train infantry units for typical combat situations, the 2nd Iron Brigade Combat Team from 1st US Armored Division "Old Ironsides", which is based in Baumholder, Germany, held Exercise "Magic Trap 2001". This field training exercise was held from 27 November to 3 December 2001 in the region of Kusel/Steinbach. The main participants in the exercise were two mechanized infantry battalions of the 2nd Iron Brigade Combat Team: the 1st Bn, 6th Infantry Regiment (1-6INF) "Regulars" and the 2nd Bn, 6th Infantry Regiment (2-6INF) "Gators".

Because of heavy rain at the time and swampy ground, the first part of the exercise, the deployment of M1A1HA Abrams Main Battle Tanks from 1st Bn, 35th Armored Regiment, was cancelled.

Infantry Warfare in Unknown Terrain

Exercise "Magic Trap 2001" began in the early morning of 27 November 2001 with the deployment of the combat companies of 1st Bn and 2nd Bn of the 6th Mechanized Infantry Regiment. The units deployed from their bases in Baumholder and traveled by road to the training area between Kusel and Ramstein, west of Autobahn A62 near the towns of Konken, Wahnwegen, Steinbach, and Pettersheim. After the units had arrived at the training area, they began to train on a platoon level.

The weather conditions during Exercise "Magic Trap 2001" were very bad. Heavy rain, typical for middle Europe in the last days of autumn, taxed soldiers and vehicles to their limits. Heavy terrain and swampy ground do not allow for mistakes when driving. If the bottom of the Bradley's hull is sucked into the wet ground, only another Bradley or a recovery tank can free the vehicle.

The M2A2 ODS Bradley is the workhorse of today's US Army mechanized infantry battalions. The improved ODS version was introduced in 1997. The first vehicles were delivered in that year to units of the 3rd US Infantry Division.

Every company was responsible for the planning and controlling of several different training scenarios. The training for each platoon was divided into different parts containing a variety of combat situations, and it was up to each platoon to successfully resolve each part. All the training was geared toward making use of the capabilities of the newest version of the Bradley AFV, the M2A2 ODS (Operation Desert Storm).

The training focused on the following:

- Taking advantage of the high mobility and protection of the Bradley ODS
- Fighting mounted from the vehicle using the 25mm main gun and dismounted with the Bradley ODS in the support role
- Clearing mines and opening minefields for the passage of heavy vehicles
- Getting over barbed wire obstacles with the support by tracked vehicles

Armored combat teams fight with high mobility, but blind terrain forced the infantry to dismount from their "battle taxis". The MICV Bradley is designed to transport the infantry soldiers as near as possible to their dismount point. When the infantrymen leave the vehicle, they will be protected by the heavy weapons of the Bradley: the 25mm Bushmaster electric gun, the coaxial 7.62mm machine gun M240C, and the TOW.

"Broken Track". The repair of a broken track demands a lot of sweat and muscle power, but it is a typical job for a Bradley crew. Often the vehicle with a broken track is disabled and ends up in a ditch.

- Clearing and guarding captured terrain with a mechanized infantry platoon.

Some Bradley ODS vehicles acted in the OPFOR (Opposing Force) role using the new Precision Gunnery System (PGS) gunfire simulator. This training system is similar to the AGDUS training system of the German *Bundeswehr*. In addition, all soldiers and tracked vehicles that took part in "Magic Trap 2001" were fitted with the MILES II training system.

During the exercise, the troops used night vision equipment and

newly introduced small arms like the M4A1 carbine, M16A4 assault rifle and M240B medium machine gun. Most weapons were upgraded with laser pointers, telescopic sights, etc. Umpire and controller teams riding in HMMWV wheeled vehicles observed the different training stations and provided "After Action Review" (AAR) to the soldiers. This review served to point out faults and mistakes, but at the same time good ideas and performance were recognized.

When a platoon performed well and the umpires agreed with the results, the platoon could advance to the next station. This rotation from one training station to the next was planned out exactly. If a platoon made

To prevent casualties from "friendly fire", the M2A2 ODS Bradleys of 1st and 2nd Bns, 6th INF are fitted with the so-called Friend Foe Panels (IFF) on the vehicle's rear, sides and turret frontplates. The short antenna near the rear right light is a sensor for directing the vehicle's travel. Its data is transferred to the new AN/PSV-11 Portable Lightweight GPS Receiver (PLGR).

In addition to the Friend Foe Panels (IFF), this Bradley from 2-6INF is marked with an orange cloth (normally used to assure identification by friendly aircraft). During the Gulf War, some Bradleys were lost to "friendly fire", mainly when hit by the 120mm main gun of an M1A1 Abrams MBT.

"Dark Assault". A Bradley platoon undertakes an attack operation in the typical autumn fog on a November morning in 2001. Following current US Army tactical doctrine, Mechanized Infantry Fighting Vehicles (MICV) like the Bradley will always deploy together with an M1A1 Abrams MBT.

The ODS version of the Bradley is based on the A2 version, but with a redesigned hull and external armor plates around the hull and turret. The eyelets on the side armor plates are used to attach personal gear, roles of barbed wire or rucksacks. A water canister can be fitted behind the black rubber flap.

too many mistakes at a station, the umpires decided that the platoon had to do the job again in a better manner. Because of bad weather and heavy rain, the whole exercise was terminated on 3 December, and the units redeployed to their bases in Baumholder.

This type of exercise has proven itself over the past ten years with units rotating at CMTC Combat Maneuver Training Center, Hohenfels, Germany. But the soldiers there know every tree and stone in the area. So "Magic Trap 2001" was a treat for the troops since they could train in unknown terrain. For the 2nd Iron Brigade Combat Team, this exercise was the first one held on open ground since the last FTX in 1989. These facts made "Magic Trap 2001" very important, effective and valuable for the participating units of the 2nd US Iron Brigade Combat Team.

Organization of a Mechanized Infantry Unit

The structure of a US Army mechanized infantry battalion has changed very often in recent decades. Each time, the structure was a result of actual tactical requirements. Today a typical mechanized infantry battalion in the 1st US ID ("Big Red One") and 1st US AD ("Old Ironsides") based in Germany has the following structure:

The battalion has three mechanized combat companies equipped with

Bradley M2A2 ODS vehicles. Each mechanized infantry combat company is divided into four platoons: the 1st, 2nd, 3rd platoon and the company headquarters platoon. The company has a strength of 14 Bradley M2A2 ODS and one M113A3, supported by a pair of 5-ton cargo trucks and two HMMWVs. The three platoons each have four Bradley M2A2 ODS and are the backbone of the company. The platoon itself is the smallest operational unit when building combat teams. The company headquarters platoon has two Bradley M2A2 ODS for the company commander (CO) and company executive officer (XO), and the wheeled vehicles are used for support and liaison.

In the structure of the mechanized infantry battalion, the battalion adds its own headquarters company. In this large and complexly structured organization you find the soldiers and vehicles of the battalion's Tactical Operation Center (TOC), the small command group with two M2A2 ODS (for the battalion commander and the battalion executive officer) and four support vehicles. The mortar platoon, the battalion's own scout platoon, and the medical platoon are three more elements of the battalion headquarters company. The TOC is based on the M1068 digital command post tracks (upgraded M577A2) and provides the battalion commander and his staff with tools for planning and coordination when the battalion is on exercise or combat missions.

The Bradley driver sits below a huge, heavy hatch. This hatch is the only one on the vehicle that can be opened from the outside. Because of this, the driver received the nickname "the one with the key" from his comrades.

Another improvement of the ODS Bradley version is the modification of the engine access door. Now an electro-hydraulic lift mechanism raises and lowers the huge door quickly and easily. The VTA-903 engine with its 608hp is built by Cummins.

To create more room for seven fully equipped soldiers in the cramped crew compartment of the M2A2 ODS Bradley, personal gear like rucksacks, isomats and extra boots are attached to the eyelets on the sides of the vehicle. The men have more room inside, but there is the disadvantage of the gear going unprotected against the weather and dust.

The medical platoon uses three M577A2 treatment vehicles with medical equipment, six M113A3 ambulance vehicles and three wheeled vehicles as the basic element for quickly providing first aid on the battlefield.

Finally, the mortar platoon gives the battalion indirect fire support with their four M1064A3 mortar carriers.

In total, a typically structured mechanized infantry battalion has a full strength of 104 vehicles. They are: 44 M2A2 ODS Bradley, 10 M113A3, four M577A2 Command Post, four M1064A3 mortar carriers, four M1068 digital command post tracks, 26 HMMWVs in different versions, and twelve M923 5-ton trucks.

System Description of the M2A2 ODS (Operation Desert Storm) Bradley

The new version of the well-known Bradley IFV is the M2A2 ODS. This IFV is the backbone of the 1st and 2nd Battalions of the 6th Mechanized Infantry Regiment. In mobility, agility and cross-country driving, the M2A2 ODS Bradley is equal to the M1A1HA Abrams MBT.

This photo shows two M88A1 recovery tanks of the Headquarters & Headquarters Company (HHC), maintenance platoon, 2nd Bn, 6th INF, driving through a small German town. In recovery operations, the 52-ton M88A1 can pull vehicles weighing up to 65 tons. On swampy ground and when operating with the main winch, the vehicle is stabilized with the front dozer blade.

The M88A1 has a crew of four: the driver, commander and two mechanics. The vehicle is equipped with various tools for recovery-and-repair situations. They include tow bars, welding equipment, a hydraulic cutter, and a fuel pump for fuel transfer from one vehicle to another. The A-boom on the roof can be erected hydraulically for crane operations to lift turrets or engines.

This M1064A3 Mortar Carrier from the mortar platoon of HQ Company, 2-6INF played the role of an OPFOR vehicle. This special vehicle is not fitted with the mortar base plate on the side of the vehicle or the trim vane on the front. The M1064A3 Mortar Carrier is not equipped with smoke dischargers on the front of the vehicle beneath the headlights.

The M2A2 ODS Bradley operates and fights as a member of the so-called Combined Arms Team together with the Abrams main battle tank. One possible structure of a Combined Arms Team is the "mech-heavy team". In the "mech-heavy team", two mechanized infantry platoons are reinforced by one armored platoon with four M1A1HA tanks. The 1st Bn and 2nd Bn, 6th Mechanized Infantry Regiment received their new M2A2 ODS Bradley IFVs in mid-2000. The Cummins VTA-903T turbo-charged diesel engine with 14.3 l cubic capacity and 608 hp give the 29.9-ton heavy tank a top speed of 56 km/h (35mph).

The hull of the Bradley is of welded construction using aluminum plates. The manufacturer, United Defense, reports that the Bradley is well protected against 95% of all possible ballistic threats on the battlefield. The interior of the M2A2 ODS is covered with "liner armor" to protect against splinters and artillery fragments when the vehicle is hit. A fire-fighting device is installed in both the crew compartment and the engine compartment.

The Bradley M2A2 ODS is armed with the 25mm M242 Bushmaster Electric Gun produced by McDonnell Douglas, a coaxial mounted 7.62mm machine gun and the double TOW launcher with two TOW-2 (Tube-launched, Optically-tracked, Wire-guided) anti-tank missiles. The TOW can operate up to a distance of 3750 meters (5000 yards). The soldiers in the infantry squad in the Bradley's rear compartment have

A close-up view of an M113A3 Ambulance belonging to the medical platoon of HHC 2-6INF. Following the rules of the Geneva Convention, all ambulance vehicles must be marked with big red cross on a white background and must be unarmed. Also, it is strictly forbidden to shoot ambulances or medics. In the rear compartment of the M113A3 there is space for four stretchers or eight sitting casualties.

A rare photo of an M577A2 Command Post Carrier. This vehicle is still painted in the old US Army standard European camouflage, which was commonly seen during the decade of 1980-1990. Sometimes vehicles painted in this scheme come from the former REFORGER POMCUS storage depot, but they are soon repainted in the three-color NATO camouflage scheme.

"Battle Taxi of the US Mechanized Infantry- Then and Now". Until the mid-1980s, the M113 was the standard personnel carrier for the US army mechanized infantry units. With the introduction of the M2 Bradley, the US Army received its first real Mechanized Infantry Combat Vehicle.

"Rock 6". This M1025 Armament Carrier is the vehicle used by the commander of Charlie Company. ("Rock" is the nickname of Charlie Company, 6INF). Usually the M1025 version of the Humvee, with the hard top, is used by the battalion's scout platoon.

access to additional anti-tank weapons like two Javelins and three AT-4s. The Javelin and the AT-4 replaced the Dragon and LAW missiles when the M2A2 ODS was delivered to the units.

The redesigned and upgraded M2A2 ODS is a result of the lessons learned over the past decade. A two-phase modernization of the M2A2 became necessary after experiences during Operation Desert Storm revealed some flaws. The important "first round hit" capability is increased by the newly installed laser range finder. The ODS vehicles are equipped with the GPS/POSNAV navigation system, which enhances the ability to maneuver with other members of the Combined Arms Team. The survivability of the crew and vehicle was increased with the introduction of the Battlefield Combat Identification System and a Missile Countermeasure Device. But neither system is fitted into the Bradley in peacetime or during exercises.

The infantry squad compartment in the rear of the vehicle is fitted with better designed seats for a quick and easy dismount and remount of the soldiers and their gear. The M2A2 ODS has enough growth potential for any future fitting of the most up-to-date communication and data transfer technology to fulfil the requirements of the "Force XXI" concept. In particular, the Force XXI Battle Command, Brigade and Below (FBCB2), Command and Communication (C2) requirements will make it

possible for the crews to hand over targets to other AFV's, like Bradleys, Abrams MBTs, artillery systems, and helicopters. But the introduction of this real-time-operating data link system will depend on future threats.

Operational Conception

The Bradley M2A2 ODS is one of the main elements of the concept of the Combined Arms Team, which was designed to build close cooperation with the M1A1HA Abrams main battle tank. There are four primary tasks for the Bradley:
- Provide fire support to the dismounted operating infantry
- Destroy enemy armor over long distances with the TOW system
- Destroy enemy infantry fighting vehicles and light armor vehicles
- Operate as a battle taxi to transport sufficient infantrymen, under protection, to the dismount point on the battlefield

With its arms, the 25mm Bushmaster chain gun, the TOW missile launcher for the upgraded TOW-2B missiles, and the coaxial mounted machine gun, as well as its transport capacity of seven fully equipped infantrymen in the rear compartment, the ODS Bradley can fulfil all the requirements of its main missions. There are now seven seats for the infantrymen in the redesigned rear compartment, according to the "three by nine" concept for the mechanized infantry platoon. Each vehicle carries a crew of three (commander, gunner, driver) and the nine infantrymen of the infantry squad. But there is not enough space to transport a whole squad in one Bradley. Currently, four Bradleys transport three squads (27 infantrymen). To provide the infantry squad with better information about

Here is a typical example of the omnipresent Humvee. The M998 Four-Man, Soft Top version of the Humvee was the first type delivered to the US forces in 1987. In addition to the four soldiers, more equipment, material or gear can be transported in the rear cargo area. Notice that the soft top is also painted in the 3-tone NATO camouflage. The reflectorized yellow-red plates were mounted on these military vehicles to make them more visible when driving on German civil roads.

Another variant of the 26 Humvees used in a US mechanized infantry battalion. This photo shows an M998 Two-man Cab with a large canvas cover, which is also painted in NATO camouflage. The driver's door features the distinctive X-shaped pattern that is common to the vehicle.

"Bring up the beans and bullets". This M923 cargo/personnel dropside (6x6) 5-ton truck of 2-6INF delivers hot meals to the assembly area of B Company. A mechanized infantry battalion has twelve 5-ton cargo trucks.

An Oshkosh 10-ton (8x8) HEMTT (Heavy Expanded Mobility Tactical Truck) support vehicle, seen here in the M977 cargo version. These trucks have excellent mobility in heavy terrain and can supply an infantry battalion near the front line with all needed material.

the things happening outside of their "battle taxi", a daytime camera display screen is mounted near the squad leader's seat.

With the capabilities of its weapons, its updated fire control system with the laser range finder, its improved navigation systems, and latest communication and data link systems, the ODS Bradley enables its crew to carry out high-tech operations whether they are attacking, defending against the enemy, or securing terrain. The units can operate in more dispersed, non-linear conditions whenever possible, but also as a strong formation with an impressive anti-tank capability when concentrated. Transported by C-5 or C-17 aircraft, they can be deployed for rapid reaction operations to anyplace in the world.

Units of the 2nd Iron Brigade Combat Team
1st US Armored Division "Old Ironsides"
- 1st Bn, 6th Infantry Regiment (1-6INF) with M2A2 ODS Bradley IFV
- 2nd Bn, 6th Infantry Regiment (2-6INF) with M2A2 ODS Bradley IFV

- 1st Bn, 35th Armored Regiment (1-35AR) with M1A1HA Abrams MBT
- 4th Bn, 27th Field Artillery Regiment (4-27FA) with M109A6 Paladin SPG
- 40th Combat Engineer Battalion

The so-called "Camelback" hydration system located in the rucksack was adopted from the Ranger units, and it is possible that it will replace the water bottle in the near future. The Camelback enables a soldier to drink without taking his hands from his weapon. The pictured soldier has an AN/PVS-14 night vision system attached to his helmet. When not in use, it can be flipped upwards. The soldier is armed with the modern M-16A4 rifle, an upgraded version of the proven M-16A2. Noteworthy modifications are the removable front handle and the integrated rail mounting system for different sights. Fire distance, ratio and ammunition are still the same as the M-16A2.

Two men per infantry squad carry the M249 Squad Automatic Weapon (SAW). The M249 SAW is based on the Belgian FN Minimi light machine gun. The SAW has a caliber of 5.56mm and can fire the same NATO standardized ammunition as the M-16 rifle. The 5.56mmx45mm NATO cartridge has a range of up to 800 meters (874 yards). The M249 SAW has a rate of fire of 750 rounds per minute.

Today the M240B Medium Machine Gun has replaced the aged ground-mounted M60 machine gun. The new, highly reliable weapon uses the 7.62mm round, which brings more energy to the target than the smaller 5.56mm caliber rounds of the M249 SAW.

This close-up photograph of an infantry soldier gives a good view of the MILES II equipment. The "buttons" on the gear and helmet are the sensors for the MILES II laser.

In 1973, the Syrian troops operated very successfully against the Israeli tank formations. The famous Soviet "Sagger" anti-tank missile was a nightmare for the Israeli tank crews. The American answer to the Soviet wire-guided anti-tank weapon is the Dragon. The wire-guided Dragon will be replaced in the near future by the improved Javelin anti-tank system, which is a "fire and forget" anti-tank weapon.

As dangerous as a snake in the jungle – the sniper. Here a sniper from 2-6INF is shown wearing the typical "Ghillie suit" camouflage dress. The sniper is armed with the M24 Sniper Weapon System (SWS). In the configuration shown here, the M24 (SWS) represents a combination of the M700 Remington rifle and the M40X custom trigger. The M24 (SWS) fires the 7.62mm M118 sniper round and the rounds are loaded into a 6-round integral magazine. The M24 (SWS) replaced the old M21, which was introduced in 1969.

1/35 AH-64A Apache

Italian C1 Ariete MBT
Mainstay of the Ariete Armored Brigade

Alberto Scarpitta

The insulating thermal jacket that surrounds the barrel of the 120/44 gun creates the impression of a superior caliber weapon. The jacket minimizes the distortion that occurs during firing due to differential expansion of the steel.

In the early 1980s, the Italian Army was looking for a new main battle tank to replace the 300 aging M-60A1s in use in the five battalions of the Ariete armored division, the unit that was defending the northeastern border of the country. The older American tanks had to be passed down to second-line units who were at that moment still equipped with the obsolete M-47. A first possibility was to produce under licence the German Leopard 2, for a total of 200-300 vehicles, but the Army preferred to issue a broad specification for a new tank, named *Tricolore*, to be designed and built in Italy.

The SFIM stabilized panoramic periscope enables the commander to view the entire battlefield, separate from the gunner, while continuing to direct the firing of the main gun.

This view of the Ariete tank provides a good look at the stowage boxes at the rear of the turret.

Clear view of the top of the turret showing additional armor and the MG-42/59 machine gun installed on the loader's circular guide.

Along with the 120mm gun, the tank is also armed with one 7.62mm machine gun fitted alongside the main armament and another positioned on a flexible mount on either the gunner's or commander's hatch.

In 1984, Otobreda Division of *Alenia Difesa* and the Defense Vehicles Division of Iveco formed a consortium to develop a new family of wheeled and tracked vehicles for the Italian Army, the B1 Centauro Tank Destroyer, the C1 Ariete MBT and the VCC-80 Dardo IFV. In the same year, the Army's overall specification had been agreed upon by the industry and the design work began on many components and systems. Otobreda had overall responsibility to develop the project of the C1 MBT, with Iveco providing the powerpack, the suspension system and other automotive components.

The first prototype of the new main battle tank, now called Ariete ("ram" in Italian), the same name as the most important armored unit of the Army, was completed in 1986. It was followed by the others in 1988 in order to allow the Italian Army to begin a complete program of trials. As a result, an initial order for 200 tanks was placed, to be followed by a second lot for a further 200 vehicles of an improved version.

The end of the Cold War and financial difficulties led to the cancellation of the second lot, while the production commenced with a low rate at the Otobreda facility in La Spezia in 1995 only.

The first production Ariete was completed at the end of 1995 and by 1998 the *32° Reggimento Carri* (tank regiment, a battalion-size unit) of Tauriano was entirely equipped with

Every tank regiment of the Ariete Armored Brigade fields 54 tanks, making a total of 162 MBTs. Fitted on the front plate of the hull are ice cleats that are used to prevent the tracks from slipping on ice.

This photo shows to advantage the long turret of the Ariete with its sloped front and prominent rear bustle and vertical end.

The commander's stabilized periscope is also installed on the Centauro heavy armored car, as seen in this photo.

the new MBT. Production was completed by early 2002 at a total program cost of around 970 million US dollars.

The Tank

The Ariete is a tank of classic conception and design, with posterior motor, the driver seated in the front right of the hull, and a large turret that accommodates three men: gunner and tank commander in tandem, on the right, and the loader on the left. The vehicle is made of all-steel welded construction with special composite armor on the hull front, turret front and sides. This additional protection, made of a variety of different materials ranging from metal alloys to ceramics, all encased in a steel armored box, offers considerably greater resistance and survivability than conventional highly tempered steel plates and is very effective against shaped-charge weapons. When a shaped-charge warhead explodes, all the energy is channelled by an integral cone as a jet of extremely hot gasses that cut through conventional armor. Special armor breaks and dissipates the force of the gas jet. The efficacy of the protection is then augmented by the emphatic inclination of the armour, especially on the front part of the hull and the turret.

Two armor-and-rubber side skirts produced by the firm Lasar protect the

An AB-205A utility helicopter of the Italian Army flies over a line of tanks. Visible in the foreground is the blade of a Leopard recovery vehicle.

The Ariete has a fording depth of 1.25 meters (4 feet) without special equipment. The mobility is similar to that of the Leopard 1 and will be increased by the new 1600 HP engine that will be installed soon.

top of the tracks against shaped-charge weapons and reduce the cloud of dust produced by movement. The roof of the turret has an additional layer of protection against the effect of top-attack antitank weapons, while the interior of the crew space is covered with a spall liner, which serves an anti-fragment function, and blow-up panels that vent any secondary explosion away from the turret. The overall level of protection is similar to that of the first versions of other second-generation Western tanks, like the Leopard 2A4 and Abrams M-1, but surely inferior to that of their more updated versions. This could represent one of the critical aspects of the

Italian tank, even though it is said there would be an increase in the level of protection in the frontal arc with additional external explosive-reactive add-on armor.

Obviously, Ariete has a complete system of NBC protection, an SP-180 pack manufactured by Sekur, and an automatic fire-suppressant system that works in the combat space and in the engine compartment. Adding to the survivability of the vehicle and its crew is the presence of two 80mm Galix rocket launchers of French production. Along with an anti-personnel grenade for close defense, they can fire smoke grenades that form a heavy smokescreen to confuse and blind enemy gunners. The FUM-B grenade is effective both in the visual field and in the infrared spectrum. The Galix system also works automatically in the input of the laser warning sensor mounted just ahead of the loader's hatch, which indicates when the tank is "illuminated" from an external source.

The mobility of the Ariete, not completely satisfying and similar to

The volunteers selected for tank regiments move on to the Cavalry (tank) Corps School at Lecce where they are trained on Ariete tanks. The first unit to receive the new tank was the 32nd Tank Regiment (32° Reggimento Carri), followed by the 132nd. The C1 tank has a height to the turret top of 250 cm (8.2 feet) and 285 cm (9.4 feet) to the top of the commander's periscope.

Thanks to its advanced fire control system, the tank can fire on the move with great precision.

that of Leopard 1, is provided by a supercharged Fiat/Iveco V-12 MCTA diesel engine of complete Italian design. It is a 12-cylinder, V-form, 4-stroke type that can develop 1275 HP. It is coupled with a ZF LSG-3000 automatic transmission, manufactured under license by Iveco, with four forward speeds and two reverse speeds. The maximum road speed is about 65 km/h (40mph) and it has a range of 550km (342 miles) on road. The relatively small HP that the engine produces makes the Ariete possess a weight/power ratio inferior to other latest MBTs.

The Ariete's suspension is a classic torsion bar type with seven rubber-tire road wheels, with an idler at the front and drive wheel at the back, plus four track-return rollers. Five of the seven road wheels, to be precise the first three and the last two, have hydraulic shock absorbers, while all seven suspension arms have hydraulic bumpers fitted to limit excessive travel. This layout allows for the maximum supporting surface for the tracks, making for notable qualities of elasticity. Thanks to the long vertical travel of the road wheels, whose elevated number gives an excellent distribution of weight on the tracks, and good capacity for absorbing the roughness of terrain, the crew finds itself in a particularly comfortable environment. The high

absorption capacity of the shock absorbers rapidly annuls the swings involved in firing.

Armament and Combat Equipment

The main gun that arms the Ariete is a .44-caliber 120mm smoothbore gun built by OTO Melara in La Spezia. It is fully stabilized by hydraulic servos and has the same characteristics of the guns in the Leopard 2 and M-1A1/A2 Abrams. Turret traverse and weapon elevation is effected mechanically through an electro-hydraulic system or manually in the event of damage.

The four-tank platoon moves into sections of two. When one section moves, the other protects the movement and provides a base of fire, then the roles are switched.

Tanks of the 32nd Tank Regiment maneuver in sections as they advance across the terrain at the Celline-Meduna training range in northeastern Italy.

The gun, which is equipped with a bore evacuator, muzzle reference system and thermal sleeve, can fire the same types of ammunition as the other NATO's. One is the DM-33 Armor Piercing, Fin-Stabilized, Discarding Sabot Tracer (APFSDS-T) round with a kinetic energy penetrator for antitank use. It has a weight of 23 kg (51 lb) and a muzzle velocity of 1650 m/sec (5414 f/sec). Another is the DM-12 multi-role High Explosive, Anti-Tank, Tracer, Multi-Role (HEAT-T-MP) round, which has a muzzle velocity of 1140 m/sec (3740 f/sec) and a weight of 24.5 kg (54 lb). With its special features it is suitable for both anti-tank and anti-infantry work and against less-protected targets. Forty-two rounds are carried, 15 of which are stored in the turret for immediate use and 27 are positioned beside the driver. This ammunition was produced by the firm SNIA-BPD under license from the German Rheinmetall GmbH. In 2001, the Italian Army adopted some new rounds: the CL-3143 APFSDS-T and

Ariete tanks go on the move to reach their position at the beginning of a firing exercise. The vehicle can reach a road speed of about 65 km/h (40 mph).

When not in use, the gunner's sight is protected by armored covers. Fire control and sight systems are extremely expensive, representing a large percentage of the total cost of the tank.

the CL-3105 HEAT-MP-T, produced by the Israeli Military Industries, and the Rheinmetall GmbH DM-38 APFSDS-T. The older DM-33 are to be converted into drill-rounds for training purposes.

Two 7.62mm MG-42/59 light machine guns complete the armament, one being coaxial with the gun and the other being installed on the turret, either in correspondence with the tank commander's hatch or at the loader's hatch, as desired, since both positions are equipped with an apposite circular guide. This latter machine gun can be operated from the outside only.

Ariete tanks are equipped with an advanced TURMS OG-I4 L3 main battle tank fire control and sighting system developed by Officine Galileo. This very modern computerized fire control system includes a ballistic computer, day/night sights and a laser rangefinder. It is in line with the most recent foreign developments and may constitute the most advanced aspect of the Ariete MBT.

The tank commander has a primary SFIM SP-T-694 panoramic, roof-mounted, stabilized periscope (magnification of x 2.5 and x 10). It makes it possible to observe the battlefield independently from the position of the turret, day or night, thanks to a third-generation image intensifier tube, and it does not require any infrared or other artificial light source. Once it finds a target, the commander automatically passes it to the gunner, the turret is aligned, and surveillance and search is immediately resumed. It is interesting that such freedom of action, which means better control of the external situation and quicker reaction to fire, does not exist in the early versions of second-generation tanks, for example, the American M-1A1 Abrams, which fought in Iraq in 1991.

The gunner uses a stabilized panoramic day/night sight, which offers x 5 magnification, with a laser rangefinder and thermal sight for night vision. The thermal sight can read the difference in temperature of objects in the field of view. The laser rangefinder, which is linked to a Marconi Cosmo ballistic computer, muzzle reference system and wind sensors, provides basic range information. Neither darkness of night, dust storms

The 32nd Tank Regiment has about fifty female soldiers serving in many different military occupations. Their presence is destined to grow in the future in the sectors of administration and logistics, as well as in the combat units.

nor chemical smoke screens can prevent the gunner from acquiring his target. The gunner's thermal sight picture and all-ballistic data are also transferred to the tank commander's sight.

The digital ballistic computer processes the data supplied from several sensors, and the gunner or commander, and furnishes the aiming parameters automatically, with a high probability of a "bull's eye", even when the tank is moving. The gunner has a backup sight, available in case of damage to the main system, the Officine Galileo C-102 coaxial telescope, with x 8 magnification, and three manually selectable aiming reticules.

The crew has many periscopes at its disposal for checking on the situation outside. The driver, who is seated in a hydraulically adjustable seat with a single-piece hatch, has three periscopes, the central of which

Each tank regiment fields 54 Arietes, plus a complement of logistic vehicles. This female soldier is driving the regimental commander's scout car, a Land Rover Defender 90, in Kosovo, where the unit was sent on peacekeeping duties in the spring of 2002.

The mechanized infantry complement of the Ariete: the 11th Bersaglieri Regiment, which fields the VCC-1 IFV, an Italian-built advanced version of the M-113 with appliqué armor. This unit will be among the first to receive the new Dardo IFV, which is armed with a 25mm gun.

can be replaced by a MES VG/DIL 186C1 passive periscope for night driving. The commander has seven periscopes for all-around observation, while the loader has a single-piece hatch with three periscopes looking forward and to the left. All the periscopes and sights are laser-filtered to minimize the effects of enemy lasers on the crew's eyes.

The Future

The Ariete serves to overcome a longtime generation gap in the Italian Army. In order to transform a good industrial product into an excellent operative instrument, there is much required.

First of all, the Army must realize that such an advanced instrument needs greater attention at the logistic and maintenance level. It is necessary to strongly upgrade the regimental units of fuel supply and ensure that the Ariete has adequate road mobility support by acquiring a new and more capable tank-transport truck since the current ATC-81, which is used to transport the Leopard 1 and M-60A1, cannot move the heavier Ariete.

The 7.62mm MG-42/59 light machine gun is still found in the infantry units, even after the acquisition of the lighter 5.56mm Minimi.

The VCC-1 infantry fighting vehicles follow the tanks, ready to disembark their complement of bersaglieri, the Italian armored infantry. Each five-man squad has a machine gunner armed with a Minimi 5.56mm light machine gun.

The Astra SM 88.50 TIM 8x8, coupled with the French Lohr SMC 64-6.3DI trailer, will be able to move a Class 70 tank and seems to have been selected as the new Ariete prime mover. Furthermore, current Leopard 1 recovery tanks, even with improved lifting capacity of the crane, have some limitation supporting the heavy C1 vehicle, and it would be best to develop a recovery version of the Ariete.

Studies have begun as to an Ariete Mk.2, which would have a 1500 HP engine, hydropneumatic suspensions, a more advanced fire control system, increased protection, and an auto-loader for the 120mm smoothbore gun. Financial difficulties have limited these goals, and the army is now interested in increasing the power of the engine, to improve the acceleration, which currently is not all that satisfying, and to allow the installation of a kit for additional armored protection. Fiat/Iveco has developed a more powerful version of the MTCA engine with displacement augmented to 30,000 cubic centimeters and a new injection system adopting the "Common Rail" technology. It produces 1600 HP and will be installed on all the tanks as soon as they reach their next overhaul time.

The industrial agreements between Otobreda and the French group Giat to produce the Leclerc tank open interesting perspectives for the development of a command and control system for tank units. A system developed in France, which combines the performances of digital radios and apparatuses of inertial navigation and/or receivers GPS, would enable the commanders to learn the position and every tactical situation of individual tanks. That would make it possible to address the action in an optimal way and to realize integrated operations.

The Units

According to the current guidelines of the General Staff, the new tank will be assigned only to the Ariete Armored Brigade, which consists of three armored regiments: the 4th, 32nd and 132nd Tank Regiments, plus one *bersaglieri* (mechanized infantry), one self-propelled artillery and one engineering regiment.

Anti-ambush drill for the bersaglieri of the 11th Regiment. After the volunteers reach the unit, their training continues for some months before they are considered ready for out-of-area operations.

The VCC-1 IFVs have running gear and front compartment identical to M-113 armored personnel carriers. The upper walls of the crew compartment are sloped with two firing ports on each side, with observation windows above. They are armed with a 12.7mm Browning M-2 heavy machine gun, while each vehicle carries a Panzerfaust 3 short-range anti-tank weapon.

In July 2001, the 32nd Tank Regiment received about 50 female soldiers, becoming the first armored unit in the Italian Army to engage women in operative duty as tank crewmembers. Each armored regiment, commanded by a full colonel, fields 54 tanks and is formed of a Headquarters and HQ Company and one tank battalion, consisting of four tank companies, now called "squadrons" in perfect cavalry fashion, with 13 Ariete MBTs each.

The squadrons comprise three platoons of four tanks plus a command element with another Ariete. The tanks of the regiment and battalion commanders make a total of 54 vehicles per regiment and 162 for the whole brigade. With such an organization, the tank regiments will be able to participate in NATO missions undertaken by ARRC, the Quick Reaction Allied Corps inserted in the 3rd British Division. Instead, it is expected that company modules will be employed in peace-support-operation tasks.

combined-arms task force. Tanks and armored infantry units are cross-attached to form a battalion task force or a company combat team having the assets needed to accomplish a particular mission. Cross-attachment would be facilitated by remaining within the same brigade. The mechanized infantry unit assigned to Ariete Brigade is the 11th *Bersaglieri* Regiment, a battalion-size formation composed of HQ and Headquarters Company, with communication and logistics duties, and one *bersaglieri* battalion with a small staff, three mechanized infantry companies, one anti-tank company, and one heavy mortar company.

These mechanized infantry companies are quite small, with logistic and administration work mainly handled at the regimental level. They have a small HQ element of 14 men with one VCC-1 infantry fighting vehicle and some trucks, and four 22-soldier rifle platoons (each consisting of three 7-man squads, plus the platoon commander and three VCC-1s). Each

The units equipped with this sophisticated and innovative tank are composed of VSPs, Volunteers in Permanent Service, who have the ability to perform the several functions of the crew. Their initial traning consists of two months in a basic crew specialization course and another month dedicated to the transition to the new tank in the Army Tank School at Lecce. Platoon commanders are lieutenants or senior NCOs, while a sergeant or sergeant major carries out the functions of platoon second in command.

Even though tank squadrons and platoons can function alone, armored units usually operate as part of a

Live-firing training at the 11th Bersaglieri Regiment's nearest training area. The rifle is the Beretta AR-70/90, the Italian Army's standard weapon. Note the traditional capercaillie (grouse) feather in the kevlar helmets.

Even tank crewmembers of the 32nd Tank Regiment perform basic infantry tasks in Kosovo within the Italian contingent of the KFOR.

The KFOR units collect weapons during the weapon amnesty in the region. Persons who surrender weapons are not required to provide any information concerning the origin of the weapons or personal information about themselves.

The 11th *Bersaglieri* Regiment is composed of short-term volunteers who, after having passed selection, go to a training regiment to attend a 12-week basic course. Then they are transferred to the Infantry School of Cesano di Roma for the eight-week specialization stage of their training. The goal is to develop a soldier qualified to perform all the duties related to the basic tasks and who is able to operate within a team.

After completing the specialization course, the personnel are sent to the regiment – where training continues – to let them acquire greater experience in the field and teach them to operate within a platoon. Live fire and theme activities linked to peacekeeping operations fill the largest part of the training periods.

squad has a vehicle driver and gunner, plus a dismounted element of five soldiers comprised of the squad commander and four riflemen, one of which is armed with the Minimi light machine gun. The only anti-tank weapon in the squad is the Panzerfaust 3, a compact, man-portable, shoulder-fired unguided system. Available at the platoon level is a 60mm light mortar and at least one 7.62 mm MG-42/59 machine gun.

The anti-tank company has five platoons, three with six Milan medium-range guided missile systems in three squads, with each squad having one VCC-1 and two firing posts. The other two platoons field four M-113 APCs, each fitted with a TOW long-range launcher. The company, with a total of 18 Milans and 8 TOWs, is a formidable unit. The platoons can be attached to rifle companies or grouped together depending on the tactical situation.

The heavy mortar company has six 120mm weapons that fire from the M-107A1 variant of the M-113 armored personnel carrier.

The bersaglieri's Beretta AR 70/90 rifle can be fitted with a second-generation image intensifier for night operations.

A female soldier of the 32nd Tank Regiment. Note the black beret with the badge of the armored cavalry.

ISAF Force Construction Vehicles in Afghanistan

Carl Schulze

The only tracked armored personnel carrier of the entire ISAF contingent is a M113A3 belonging to the Norwegian EOD platoon of the multinational engineer battalion of ISAF. In early April the unit was deployed to Bagram airport to assist the US forces in mine clearing operations. The vehicle is fitted with a Person Mine Roller (MR) which is a countermine protection device. During mine clearing operations the Norwegian EOD platoon uses this vehicle for reconnaissance. For better surveillance the vehicle is fitted with a special TV camera system on its right side.

On the 31st of December 2001, in Kabul, the British General McColl and the Afghan interior affairs minister, Qanuni, signed the Military-Technical Agreement between the International Security Assistance Force (ISAF) and the Interim Administration of Afghanistan. The signing of the agreement marked the beginning of a peace support operation in and around Kabul with the aim of restoring peace and providing assistance for the Interim Authority Government. ISAF, the international force, consisted of troops from 19 nations. It is limited to 5,000 troops by the United Nations Security Council Resolution (UNSCR) 1386 (2001). From the signing of the Military-Technical Agreement up to the 20th of June 2002, when Turkey received command, Great Britain was the leader nation of ISAF.

Nations and Mission

Troops of nineteen nations belong to the NATO-led ISAF: Austria (55: infantry platoon, special forces, staff officers and logistic assets); Bulgaria (32: NBC defense platoon); Czech Republic (5: medical personnel); Great Britain (1514: headquarters company, infantry battalion, NBC defense element, engineer company, EOD, military police, field hospital, and logistic battalion); Denmark (45: EOD, military police and staff personnel); Finland (46: staff officers and CIMIC personnel); France (489: EOD, infantry company, armored reconnaissance company, staff officers, logistic assets); Germany (927: infantry battalion, field hospital, military police, transport helicopter asset, air transport asset); Greece (123: engineers and air transport assets); Italy (356: infantry company, military police and special forces); The Netherlands (219: infantry company, special forces and air transport assets); New Zealand (7: movement control personnel for the APOD); Norway (22: EOD and movement control personnel for the APOD); Portugal (8: medical personnel); Romania (26: military police platoon and air transport assets); Spain (351: EOD, engineer company, logistic element, staff officers; and air transport assets); Sweden (40: CIMIC personnel and staff officers); and Turkey (256:

infantry company and staff officers). The remaining 44 soldiers belong to the US armed forces and form a liaison detachment in the ISAF HQ that is responsible for the contact and co-ordination between ISAF and the US-led coalition forces of Operation "Enduring Freedom".

Most of these troops and their equipment were deployed to Afghanistan in January and February 2002. Because Afghanistan has no access to the world's oceans and Kabul is surrounded by mountains sometimes several thousand meters high, the entire deployment was accomplished by means of a massive air bridge since that was the only way to reach the city. During this time, the multinational Movement Control Center (MCC) at Kabul International Airport unloaded daily up to 35 transport aircraft ranging from the small C-160 Transall to the An-126 Antonov with its payload of 120 tons. During this period, it was not uncommon for more than 300 tons of cargo to be unloaded during a single day. Every piece of kit, all troops, all weapons, all vehicles, and all supplies were flown into Afghanistan. Both Kabul International Airport and the US airfield in Bagram were used during the deployment. Great Britain, Norway, Spain, and New Zealand provided personnel for the MCC.

The ISAF, which works closely with the United Nations and the Afghan interim government, has three principal tasks:
- aid the interim government in developing national security structures
- assist in the country's reconstruction and
- assist in developing and training future Afghan security forces.

Rules of engagement are closely linked to the terms of the Military-Technical Agreement. Under the Agreement, the ISAF has "complete and unimpeded freedom of movement throughout the territory and airspace of Afghanistan". The mission of the ISAF is limited to Kabul and its vicinity. Although Afghan Prime Minister Hamid Karzai indicated that many

Communications linking ISAF with national and international headquarters outside Afghanistan as well as with the UN are provided by Britain's 30th Signal Regiment. The regiment is the only unit in the British army fielding latest satellite communication technology. One of the RA 1601 satellite ground station antennas of the unit can be seen at the ISAF HQ in the center of Kabul. In the front a Land Rover 110 XD "Wolf" of 3rd (UK) Division Headquarters and Signal Regiment is visible. Note the 3rd (UK) Division badge worn by the standing soldier on his left sleeve.

Afghanis are eager to see international peacekeepers throughout Afghanistan, US military officials remain wary of dispatching peacekeepers to other cities while the military campaign is still ongoing. An amendment to the UN resolution would be needed to expand the ISAF operation beyond the Afghan capital.

ISAF Battle Groups

All combat troops of ISAF are under command of the Kabul Multinational Brigade (KMNB). Up until March 2002, the KMNB was led by the British Brigadier Barny White Spunner, commander of 16 Air Assault Brigade. On the 19th of March, Brigadier Spunner handed over command to the German Brigadier Carl Hubertus von Butler. The forces commanded by the KMNB include these three infantry task forces:
- German airborne infantry battalion, re-enforced by a Dutch infantry company, an Austrian infantry platoon, and a Danish EOD platoon. The Area of Responsibility of this unit consists of the center of Kabul and its eastern outskirts.
- French mechanized infantry battalion re-enforced by a platoon of the Royal Air Force Regiment. The unit is responsible for the protection of the airport and the control of the rural area north of Kabul to Bagram, an area that includes the two roads leading from Kabul to Bagram.
- British infantry battalion re-enforced by a Turkish infantry company. The AOR of this formation consists of all of western Kabul.

A twenty-two man force of Romanian military policemen is attached to the 13th Air Assault Support Regiment. The platoon regularly patrols along the main ISAF supply roads between the ISAF bases and Kabul International Airport in order to keep them open. The company is equipped with a couple of ARO 244 4x4 cross country vehicles.

battalion and the re-enforced British combat service support battalion. The multinational engineer battalion, which is led by the HQ of the British 26 Engineer Regiment, is formed of British, Greek, Italian, Norwegian, and Spanish engineer units. The troops of the British combat service support battalion are provided by 13 Air Assault Support Regiment. A Romanian military police platoon and a Bulgarian NBC defense platoon are under command of the unit. Finally, the commander of KMNB also has control of the ISAF helicopter support unit provided by the German *Heeresflieger* (Army Air Corps), which commands six CH-53G CS medium transport helicopters.

British/Turkish Battle Group

The British Forces were the first to dispatch troops under ISAF command. When the Military-Technical Agreement was signed, General McColl already had Royal Marines of 40 Commando under his command. These troops were drawn from the British element of Operation "Swift Freedom" and were soon relieved by elements of 16 Air Assault Brigade. On the 10th of January, the 2nd Bn, The Parachute Regiment was the first unit of ISAF patrolling the streets of Kabul. Some of these patrols were conducted with local policemen, and British paratroopers armed with SA-80 A2s often patrolled along with policemen armed with RPG-7 anti-tank weapons. As the Paras were only an entry force, they were relieved in February by the 1st Bn, The Royal Anglian Regiment.

This Iveco 40.10 WM ambulance of the Spanish ISAF contingent is profiled while its crew was busy providing humanitarian help in the outskirts of Kabul. Inside the vehicle there is space for up to four casualties on stretchers.

The Vamtac, based on the HMMWV, is produced by URO and is a five-ton vehicle is powered by a six-cylinder turbo-diesel engine developing 89KW providing a top speed of 130km/h. The vehicle belongs to a Spanish signal detachment which provides communication between the ISAF HQ and the Spanish ISAF contingent.

The Bulgarian NBC defense platoon is equipped with eleven trucks of various types. Here a Zil 131 6x6 in the ARS-14 decontamination truck version can be seen. The vehicle can also be used as fire fighting vehicle or water tanker.

The AOR of the battalion consists of the western part of Kabul, which shows the most destruction. The boundaries of the ISAF AORs run along the police districts of Kabul, and the British AOR comprises police districts 3, 5, 6 and 7. The three forward deployed infantry companies of the battalion usually conduct 35 to 40 patrols a week, which usually run for 3 to 4 hours. During the night, the patrols are supported with information gathered by the four observation posts of the fire support company, which are placed on high ground around the AOR. Re-enforced by soldiers of 19 Field Regiment Royal Artillery, the Royal Anglians field the latest available surveillance technology in these OPs, which includes the M-STAR target acquisition radar and the hand-held SOPHY thermal imaging scope. During the curfew, the OPs guide the patrols in the city to places where suspicious movement was reported.

The main base of the Royal Anglian Battle Group is Camp Souter on the Jalalabad road. Here the battalion's logistic assets are based, along with the fire support company. The Anglian Battle Group's weaponry consists of the standard 5.56mm SA-80A2 assault rifle, the 5.56mm LSW light machine gun and the 7.62mm GPMG machine gun. The 5.56mm MINIMI, which the Anglians also use, is new to the inventory of the British infantry and bridges the gap between the LSW and the GPMG. If necessary, the battalion can also deploy six 81mm L16 mortars, 12 Milan guided anti-tank weapon systems, as well as a huge number of LAW 80 anti-tank weapons. For mounted patrols, the "Vikings", as the 1st Battalion, The Royal Anglian Regiment is nicknamed, use either the Pinzgauer 4x4 TUM(HD) or the Land Rover Defender 110 XD. Other vehicles of the

Afghanistan is littered with over ten-million mines and countless rounds of unexploded ammunition. Most of this dangerous debris is buried in the ground along the former confrontation lines of the Soviets, the anti-Communist Mujahadeen, the Northern Alliance and the Taliban forces. Among the strongly mine poised areas are the region north of Kabul and the Bagram area. Here a Hydrema 910 mine clearing vehicle from the Norwegian EOD platoon is seen in action on Bagram airport. The vehicle uses a rotating flail system with a width of 3.4 meters and can clear a path of up to three kilometers in one hour.

battalion include the Reynolds Boughton RB-44 2-ton truck and the Bedford 4x4 4-ton truck.

Before Turkey took over as lead nation of ISAF in June 2002, a company of Turkish mountain commandos was also part of the Royal Anglian Battle Group. The 250-soldier company was responsible for police district 1. Its entire vehicle fleet consisted of Land Rover-based transports built under license by the Turkey-based company Otokar. Among these were four Otokar armored patrol vehicles and one Otokar Akrep light reconnaissance vehicle, as well as several Land Rover 110 troop carriers. The weaponry of the Turkish company consisted of a mix of Eastern and Western models, including the 7.62x51mm G3A4 assault rifle, some of which are fitted with a 40mm M203 PI grenade launcher or are used as sniper rifles with a scope. Other weapons used are the 7.62mm Dragunov SVD sniper rifle and the 7.62mm PK machine gun.

French Battle Group
The main mission of the 500-man French battalion, called BATFRA, is to provide security for Kabul International Airport and the two roads linking Kabul with Bagram. Due to this mission, the French AOR is the largest within ISAF, stretching 50km by 30km between Kabul and

As liaison the Norwegian EOD platoon uses the armored version of the Mercedes G cross country vehicle. Together with the Hydrema 910 mine clearing vehicle these Mercedes took part in the de-mining operation carried out on the Bagram airport in order to improve the safety along the runway.

The British combat service and support unit of ISAF is based in Camp "Warehouse". Basically the unit is formed by the 13th Air Assault Support Regiment Royal Logistic Corps of the 16th Air Assault Brigade. The main mission of the unit is to store and distribute supplies such as fuel, water, and food for ISAF troops.

A photograph of one of a fleet of Leyland Medium Mobility Load Carrier (MMLC) vehicles belonging to the 13th Air Assault Support Regiment Royal Logistic Corps. The MMLC is fitted with the Demountable Rack Offload and Pickup System (DROPS). In the logistical area of military operations DROPS and similar systems have significantly reduced the number of needed vehicles while maintaining the same transport capacity. In addition the time of loading and unloading also lowered, as with DROPS the hull flat rack is dropped and the truck can just load another flat rack using the automatic loading system.

A Caterpillar Deployable Universal Combat Earthmover (DEUCE) in action on Kabul International Airport. Several DEUCE vehicles were purchased by the British army prior to the Afghanistan deployment and the vehicle saw action for the first time with British engineers during the rebuild of Kabul airport. The fifteen-ton heavy DEUCE features a hydraulically operated dozer blade, a six-ton winch, hydraulic tool connections and hydraulic tool set, hook and towing lugs.

Bagram. It covers about 50 villages with a majority of Pashtun inhabitants but with Tadjik administrations. The battalion is composed of the battalion staff with a signals platoon, a support company, and an infantry company of the 21ème *Régiment d'Infanterie de Marine* (RIMa – Marines). In addition to these, the battalion staff commands a light armored reconnaissance company of the 1er *Régiment de Spahis* and a company of airborne engineers of the 17ème *Régiment du Génie Parachutiste*, as well as a platoon of 34 Squadron Royal Air Force Regiment with 36 British soldiers.

The eight soldiers of an infantry section of the 17 RIMa are armed with six 5.56mm FAMAS F1 assault rifles, one 5.56mm MINIMI light machine gun, one 7.62mm N AAT mle F1 machine gun, AT 4 hand-held anti-tank weapons, and rifle grenades to be fired by the FAMAS. A platoon of 17 RIMa numbers two of these sections and an anti-tank section armed with two ERYX guided anti-tank missile systems. The platoon HQ also comprises a sniper squad with two 7.62mm FR-F2 sniper rifles and one 12.7mm PGM Hecate.

The reconnaissance company of the 1er *Règiment de Spahis* has 26 VBL wheeled armored reconnaissance vehicles, twelve of which are

armed with the 7.62mm N AAT mle F1. Eight VBL are armed with Milan guided anti-tank missile systems, while the remaining four are fitted with an 12.7mm M2HB machine gun. The British soldiers of RAF Regiment use the common British infantry weapons, i.e., the 5.56mm SA-80A2 assault rifle, the 5.56mm LSW light machine gun, the 7.62mm GPMG machine gun, the L-96A1 sniper rifle, the 94mm LAW 80 hand-held anti-tank weapon, a 51mm mortar, and AGGS rifle grenades. For patrol duties, the British soldiers use two Land Rover "Snatch" armored vehicles.

German-Dutch-Austrian-Danish Battle Group

The "German" ISAF contingent, which is stationed in Camp "Warehouse", numbers 1100 soldiers, among them 55 Austrians, 219 Dutch and 45 Danes. Apart from the German infantry battalion, the contingent also comprises a German field hospital with the technical equipment of a civilian central hospital, a *Heeresflieger* (German Army Air Corps) contingent with six CH-53G CS transport helicopters, an engineer company that also runs the camp, a maintenance company, a support company, and a military police platoon. The German infantry battalion is composed of the HQ and support company of *Fallschirmjägerbataillon* 313 (313th Airborne Battalion) and two parachute companies of the same unit, re-enforced by a Wiesel platoon from *Fallschirmjägerpanzerabwehrbataillon* 272 (272th Airborne Anti-tank Battalion). The German AOR combines police districts 2, 4, 8, 9, 11, 12, and 15 and the Bagrami district. Basically, it runs from the northwest to the southeast right through the center of Kabul and contains the ISAF HQ, as well as most foreign embassies.

The German paras are armed with the 5.56mm G 36 assault rifle, the 9mm P8 pistol, the 7.62mm MG 3 machine gun, the 40mm HK 69A1 grenade pistol, and the 300 WinMag G 22 sniper rifle. There are twelve ATF Dingo wheeled patrol vehicles for transport purposes, as well as nine Wiesel 1 airborne weapon carriers, three of which are fitted with the TOW guided anti-tank missile system and the remaining six with a 20mm Mk.20-2 machine cannon. Other vehicles used are the 2-ton Unimog and the Mercedes G cross-country vehicle.

Austria attached a 42-soldier infantry platoon and 13 medical and staff personnel to the battle group. The Austrian infantry platoon, which combines soldiers of *Jägerbataillon* 25 (25th Infantry Battalion) and the Zentrum *Jagdkampf*, is commanded by 2nd Company of *Fallschirmjägerbataillon* 313. The Austrian soldiers are armed with 9mm Glock 17 pistols, 5.56mm Steyr AUG assault rifles (which are called Sturmgewehr 77 by the Austrian army), 7.62mm MG 74 machine guns, a version of the MG 3, and the 7.62mm SSG 69 sniper rifle. Along with

Engineers from the 36th Engineer Regiment build a wall of HESCO bastion containers—made from wire mesh the containers are filled with gravel and then provide protection against small arms fire and artillery shrapnel. The vehicle is a Volvo F 10 6x6 tipper with crane. Like seen in the picture the crane can be fitted with an excavator bucket.

This Leyland 4x4 5 ton truck belongs to the 13th Air Assault Support Regiment Royal Logistic Corps, which can be noted by the black and red square painted to the vehicle front, resembling the unit Drop Zone (DZ) flash.

Followed by a VBL armored reconnaissance vehicle a Greek Volvo FM 12 dump truck transports gravel for building field fortifications. Note that the windscreen of the vehicle is protected against the impact of stones by mesh wire, a practice which is common on military vehicles taking part in peace support operations.

security tasks, the Austrian soldiers also perform patrol duties, for which they have Pandur four-wheeled armored personnel carriers and 16 Puch G cross-country vehicles. The soldiers of the Zentrum *Jagdkampf* are also tasked with special operations and VIP protection.

The majority of the 220-soldier Dutch ISAF contingent comes from the *Korps Commando Troepen* and the 13th Infantry Battalion "*Stootstroepen*", which is part of the 11 *Luchtmobile Brigade* (11th Airmobile Brigade). The Dutch company is under command of the German 313th Airborne Battalion and its AOR combines police districts 8 and 12 with the Bagrami district. The Dutch soldiers are armed with the 9mm Glock 17 pistol, the 5.56mm C7A1 assault rifle and the 5.56mm C8A1 carbine, both manufactured by Diemaco, the 7.62mm FN MAG machine gun, and the 7.62mm Accuracy International sniper rifle. Heavy weapons are the AT-4 hand-held anti-tank weapon, six TOW guided anti-tank missile systems and three 81mm mortars. The vehicle park features nine Patria Sisu XA-188 wheeled armored personnel carriers and 64 Mercedes G cross-country vehicles.

The 45-soldier Danish contingent is an EOD platoon with two MOWAG Eagle reconnaissance vehicles and all the equipment necessary for mine clearing and the disposal of other explosives. The Danish EOD specialists work closely together with their colleagues from other nations.

Not a Quiet Deployment

During their time in Kabul, the daily routine of the ISAF troops, which consisted of patrolling and manning observation posts, was often interrupted by the outbreak of violence. On the 14th of February 2002, during riots at the Kabul airport that were started by travellers on their Hadj to Mekka, the Afghan Minister of Tourism, Abdul Rachman, was killed. On the 16th of March, riots erupted outside the Kabul football stadium during the match between the ISAF team and the team of Kabul United. Being the first major sports event in Kabul for years, thousands of people tried to enter the stadium, which was already filled to the brim with 30,000 football enthusiasts. In order to prevent a panic, ISAF troops stopped further football supporters from entering the stadium, which resulted in some clashes between ISAF troops and locals. ISAF soldiers were forced to use batons and fire warning shots. Approximately 50 people were injured during the clashes, four of which were ISAF soldiers.

The ISAF troops encountered a number of other dangers during their deployment. One Afghan was killed on the 16th of February during an incident that occurred near an OP of the 2nd Battalion, The Parachute Regiment. The British soldiers manning the OP returned fire after they were engaged by small arms fire. On the 19th of February, a multinational training team of soldiers from Germany, France, the United Kingdom, Italy, the Netherlands, and Turkey began training the 1st Battalion, The Afghan National Guard. The training of the unit finished on the 3rd of

April with an official ready-for-service parade in front of the Chairman of the Interim Authority Government, Hamid Karzai.

On the 6th of March, two German and three Danish EOD team members were killed in an accident in Kabul. The soldiers were preparing an SA-3 surface-to-air missile for destruction when the missile exploded prematurely, killing the five soldiers and injuring another eight. After a strong earthquake on the evening of the 25th of March, which killed more than 800 people in the area of Nahrin, ISAF troops and US forces deployed to the region and assisted the health organizations in order to prevent a humanitarian catastrophe. During an incident on the 30th of March, an ISAF patrol managed to take two armed raiders prisoner after a firefight in western Kabul. On the 7th of April, ISAF troops came under fire by Chinese-made 107mm rockets, but the missiles missed their targets.

In June, the main task for ISAF was to provide security to the *Loya Jirga* (Grand Tribunal Council), which involved 1450 delegates from all parts of the country and took place in Kabul between the 10th and 18th of June 2002. ISAF was only responsible for the outer perimeter since the

In order to avoid the appearance of being an occupying army, ISAF mandates that the heavier weapons in its arsenal, especially those mounted on vehicles, be covered or hidden from view. This VBL wheeled armored reconnaissance vehicle belongs to the Greek engineer company and usually is fitted with a .50 caliber M2 HB heavy machine gun. The VBL has a combat weight of 3.6 tons, can reach a road speed of up to 95km/h and is fully amphibious. The crew of the vehicle consists of driver, command and machine gunner. Greece specially bought the VBL to equip its troops deployed on peace support operations with a fast and reliable wheeled armor protected reconnaissance vehicle. In addition to ISAF, Greek VBLs were deployed to Kosovo with KFOR.

Greece attached a 120-man engineer company under ISAF command. Here a platoon of the company can be seen returning from a CIMIC operation at one of the schools of Kabul to the base of the unit north of the Jalalabad road in the east of the city. The equipment of the Greek company includes heavy plant machinery and dump trucks.

Spanish troops of the MCC and the Spanish engineer company of the multinational engineer battalion just load supplies onto a Unimog U 2150L on Kabul International Airport. The key to the MCC success is to coordinate that supplies are picked up by the nation they are addressed for immediately after they have been unloaded from the transport aircraft.

The engineer equipment of the Greek company includes all types of heavy plant machinery and dump trucks. Here a WB 93 "Utility" multi purpose machine can be seen fitted with a front end loader and a hydraulic excavator. Due to the long period of war machines like this are a rarity in Kabul and often ISAF engineers support Afghan government works with their equipment, a task which is strongly related to ISAF's CIMIC activity and the best way to gain the faith of the local population.

Most of the Greek engineer company vehicles are fitted with mesh wire protection screens in front of their windscreens, like it can be seen on this 4x4 Mercedes 240 GD pick up cross country vehicle. The Mercedes GD vehicles are produced under license in Greece and over 5,000 were supplied to the Greek armed forces.

Afghan units recently trained by the ISAF provided security in the conference area. The 1st Bn, The Afghan National Guard also conducted the security checks for the people taking part in the meeting. The *Loya Jirga* made decisions for the government for the next two years and decided how the country will develop socially, politically and economically.

Mandate Extension

On the 20th of March, the United Nations Security Council extended the ISAF mandate for another six months to December 2002. But instead of contributing more troops, which would deploy outside Kabul and police the country, the focus of the UN was shifted to rebuilding Afghanistan's army and police force. It is certain that the mandate will be extended again for this reason: since the *Loya Jirga* has successfully taken place and a new government has been established in Afghanistan, there is a good chance for a lasting peace in the country in the future. But until there is a sufficient number of Afghan security forces available to protect the government and provide law and order, the international force is needed to assist the peace process.

This Pegaso 7323 six-ton fuel tanker belongs to the Spanish logistic assets and was pictured in Camp "Warehouse" while picking up supplies from Britain's 13th Air Assault Support Regiment Royal Logistic Corps. The 6x6 truck is powered by a six-cylinder turbo charged diesel engine which allows a maximum speed of 90km/h.